MY GLOBAL GOODIES

Created by :

SADHANA MISTRY

Written by :

Sadhana Mistry

e-mail : sadhanamistry@hotmail.com

Dietician :

Nimisha Shah

Graphic & Designed by :

Midas Touch, Mumbai

t. +91-22-2864 8324,
+91-22-65283618
+91-22-4016 3618

e-mail : midastuch@rediffmail.com
v.midastuch@gmail.com

Printed by :

Paras Printers, Mumbai

t. +91-22-9322661127
+91-22-28337268

First edition - Jan-2008

9 780979 283925

ISBN 978-0-9792839-2-5

Dedication :

This book I dedicate to my loving children Umang and Khushbu for their constant support.

Introduction :

Art of cooking plays a pivotal role in every one and Specially Ladies life. Everyone likes to cook, but very few people can cook well. If you enjoy cooking, you can learn it faster. If you choose the right ingredients and cook from the heart you can always cook well and then only people will enjoy your delicious food.

This book is not just another cookbook, but it is a book mastering cooking. In this book I have presented my own heart experiences, skills and ideas to make cooking Fun & Enjoying, so gct ready and get shared one by one.

I have taken every effort to keep these recipcs as simple as possible and they can be prepared in small quantities.

Kitchen King Seasoning

Ingredients :

- Cinnamon sticks - 4 oz.
- Whole clove - ½ oz.
- Bay leaves - 12 leaves
- Whole Cumin - 1 oz.
- Whole black pepper corn - 1 oz.
- Star anise - 1 oz.

Suggestion :

In this Cookbook you will need special seasoning for many recipes, you are going to have to make Kitchen King Seasoning to make your food taste real good and be satisfied.

Method :

All remain ingredients grind and make powder. Fill in one air tight jar and keep in kitchen to cook easy and for tasty food. (Also you have optional buy all remaining ingredients powder from store. Mix and fill up in the one air tight jar or container.)

Noodle Soup

Ingredients :

- 2 oz chow main noddles
- 1 medium finely chopped ripe tomato
- 2 oz cut corn
- 2 oz green peas
- 1 oz celery chopped
- 1 oz cut or shredded carrots
- 2 oz cut green onion
- Some amount of ginger paste
- Some amount of fresh cilantro cut
- Some amount of hot chilli sauce
- Few drops of fresh lemon
- Pinch of crust peppercorn
- ½ oz cube of soup
  (your choice of cube of soup)

Cooking time :

5 minutes

Tip :

If you wish to add ketchup in the soup then you always add 1 tea spoon ketchup in while it boils.

Method :

Pour three cups of water in a pot and bring to the boil. Put all the ingredients in except noodles and cube of soup. Now boiling it uncover three minutes on medium flame. Then add noodles and the cube of soup. Keep boiling for the next three minutes. Remove it from the heat. Serve hot immediately for a very fresh taste.

Vegetable Soup

Ingredients :

- 350 ml 100% vegetable juice
- 2 oz tomato puree
- 1 teaspoon whole cumin seeds
- 1/4 teaspoon garlic paste
- 1/4 teaspoon crust black pepper
- Salt to taste
- Lemon juice to taste
- Some amount of toasted bread crumbs
- Pinch of red chili powder
- ½ teaspoon butter
- 1 teaspoon olive oil

Cooking time :

5 minutes

Tip :

You can also add fresh sweet basil chopped in towards your taste.

Method :

Heat the pot on the stove on medium heat. Heat oil and butter, then crackle the cumin seeds. Put garlic paste, chili powder, and stir it for a few seconds. Pour the vegetable juice and tomato puree, black pepper, salt, and lemon juice. Add a little water. Bring it to two or three boil. serve hot in a soup bowl and top it with finely garnished bread crumbs.

Salad in Tortilla Bowl

Ingredients :

Cooking time :
20 to 30 minutes

- 6 flour tortillas
- 6 oz green cabbage finely cut
- 2 oz purple cabbage finely cut
- 3 oz mix chili finely cut (fresh jalapeno, yello bell peppers, red bell peppers)
- 1 teaspoon brown mustard
- 1¼ teaspoon of sea salt
- 2 oz green and red seedless grapes cut
- 2 oz seedless orange small pieces
- 1 oz vegetable oil
- 1 tablespoon dried Parmesan cheese
- Some amount of fresh parsley and cilantro cut
- 1 tablespoon green onion cut
- 1 oz onion slices thin
- Some amount of cucumber slices thin
- 2 oz shredded carrot
- Vegetable oil to deep fry

Method :

Heat oil in a deep saucepan on 375F, then put one tortilla in. Put one sauce ladle on tortilla. Let it fry until it is golden brown and turns into a owl shape, flip to the other side and make it golden brown as seen in the picture, fry the remaining tortilla's the same way and keep them in a plate on a side, now put all the cut vegetable's grapes and an orange in one bowl, heat one saucepan with 1 oz oil in then put mustard seeds in till they pop, then put in mixed chili in, caramelize one minute and remove this from the stove, put them in a vegetable bowl, put in salt and parmesan cheese, Toss it with a spatula, now the salad is done, put the salad in a tortilla bowl and now it's ready to eat. You can serve this as a salad or as a side dish.

Salad with black salt

Ingredients :

- 1 Medium red onion slices
- 1 Medium tomato slices
- 1 Medium cucumber slices
- ¼ teaspoon crust peppercorn
- 1 fist of amount cut cilantro and parsley
- 1/8 teaspoon black salt powder
- ¼ teaspoon roasted cumin powder
- 1 pinch of red pepper powder
- Few drops olive oil
- Few drops fresh lime

Fixing time :

5 minutes

Method :

Place, onion slices, tomato slices, and cucumber slices in a plate. Sprinkle cilantro, parsley, oil, lime, red pepper, cumin powder, black salt, and pepper corn. Then, it is ready to serve.

Green Onion Dip

Ingredients :

- 1 bunch of fresh onion cut
- 1-teaspoon fresh cilantro cut
- 2-teaspoon raw peanuts
- 1 teaspoon chopped garlic
- Salt to taste
- 1-teaspoon oil
- 1 teaspoon lemon juice

Tip :

Try to make this dip kind of chunky and not into a complete paste texture.

Method :

Put all the ingredients in the food processor and mix it. Mix it like finely chopped, Serve it with your favorite appetite.

Mint Dip

Ingredients :

- 1 bunch fresh cilantro cut
- 1 tablespoon fresh mint leaves divided
- 1-teaspoon cumin powder
- 1-teaspoon oil
- Salt to taste
- 2 teaspoon lemon juice
- 1-teaspoon garlic paste
- 2-3 hot peppers

Method :

Put all the ingredients in a mixer and make it like paste.
Serve it with barbeque or where ever it is suitable.

Tomatillos Dip

Ingredients :

10 OZ non-fat sour cream

- 1 lb tomatillos finely cut
- 1/4 teaspoon salt
- 1- teaspoon creamy peanut butter
- 3 cloves garlic chopped
- Some flakes of fresh cilantro cut
- one greet hot pepper or one green jalaoeno chopped

Fixing time :

5 minutes

Method :

Put all the ingredients in a mixing bowl and mix it well by spatula.
Then it is ready to serve with celery or with fresh vegetables and chips.

Spicy fruit dip (raita)

Ingredients :

- Some amount kiwi fruit cut
- Some amount orange cut
- 1 banana chopped
- 4 oz. plain yogurt
- 4 oz. sour cream
- ½ cup apple chopped
- ¼ -cup red and green grapes
- 1 cup broken cashew nuts
- 1 clove garlic chopped
- Pinch of red chili powder
- ¼ -teaspoon crust black pepper
- Pinch of cumin powder
- Salt to taste
- Pinch of lemon pepper
- Few fresh cilantro flakes

Fixing time :
10 minutes

Method :

Mix all ingredients together in a bowl. Serve with so many dishes, wherever it fits properly.

Vegetable pastry

Ingredients :

- ½ lb russet or red potato
- 3 oz. green fresh or frozen peas
- 3 oz. soy protein
- 2 oz. carrot cut
- ½ oz. fresh sweet basil cut
- ¼ teaspoon lemon pepper powder
- ½ teaspoon hot red chili powder
- ½ teaspoon ginger paste
- ½ teaspoons dry coriander crust
- Pinch of kitchen king
- Salt to taste
- Vegetable oil to deep fry
- 1 teaspoon lemon juice
- 8 oz. all-purpose flour
- 1 oz. vegetable (shortening)
- ¼ teaspoon salt
- 4 oz. water
- Extra flour (for dusting)

Cooking time :

15 minutes

Method:

Boil the potatoes in water, peel skin off. And cut them in tiny pieces. Steam the peas for 5-7 minutes. Heat medium saucepan on the stove and put one teaspoon oil in. put the coriander crust and make it a little brown. Put red chili powder, peas, carrots, salt, lemon pepper powder and remove the saucepan from the heat, put the potatoes in, kitchen king and stir it by the spatula. Put soy protein in a bowl and one ounce of water to make it soft. Leave them aside for two minutes and then put it in the mixture, add the basil in. mix the mixture by the spatula.

Dough :

Put flour in one mixing bowl. Put salt, vegetable shortening, lemon juice, and water, then kned the dough very well. If there is some water to add then add some. Now divide the dough into 12-15 balls. Make the ball a oval shape with a rolling pin. And spread some dust flour while it is rolling. Then put around two teaspoons of filling into the center. Fold pastry over to make a half circle and crimp the edges. Make all the remaining pastries the same way and place them in a plate aside.

Frying suggestion:

Pour oil in large heavy skillet saucepan or a deep fryer, fill no more than half full with oil, but deep-fry enough for pastry while frying. Avoid overcrowding.

Nutritive Value

ENERGY	-	422.5	KCAL
PROTEIN	-	17.9	GMS
FAT	-	11.9	GMS
FIBRE	-	4.8	GMS
SODIUM	-	23.5	MGMS
CALCIUM	-	9.2	MGMS
IRON	-	5.5	MGS
CARBOHYDRATES	-	64.0	GMS

THIS ABOVE RECIPE IS FOR 125 GMS (1SERVING) OF THE COOKED RECEIPE

Spread Sandwich

Ingredients :

- White or wheat bread slices
- 2 oz mayonnaise
- 1 oz sour cream
- 2 oz lettuce cut
- Some amount of green bell pepper cut
- Some amount of green olives
- Some amount of green onion cut
- 1-teaspoon olive oil
- Salt to taste
- 1-teaspoon garlic chopped
- Some amount of jalapenos chopped
- Some amount of red bell pepper finely cut

Fixing time :

10 minutes

Method :

Cut all side borders from the sides of the bread. Put lettuce, green bell pepper, olives, and green onions in the food processor. Make them finely chopped and squeeze all access juice from it. Then, put all of it in a bowl along with the sour cream, mayo, salt, garlic, jalapeno, red bell pepper, and oil. Mix all the ingredients very well with a spoon. Then, use a spreading knife to spread the mix on to the bread and then eat it like a sandwich.

Tahini wrap

Ingredients :

- 10 medium size flour tortillas
- 10 oz boiled chickpea
- 4 oz tahini (sesame seeds paste)
- 10 oz breaded fried onion ring
- Some amount of jalapeno slices
- Salt to taste
- 5 oz finely cut lettuce
- Some amount of salsa
- ½ teaspoon chopped garlic
- 1-teaspoon olive oil

Fixing time :

5 to 10 minutes

Nutritive Value

ENERGY	-	330	KCAL
PROTEIN	-	13.0	GMS
FAT	-	12.1	GMS
FIBRE	-	9.7	GMS
SODIUM	-	5.8	MGMS
CALCIUM	-	274	MGMS
IRON	-	3.7	MGS
CARBOHYDRATES	-	43	GMS

THIS ABOVE RECIPE IS CONSIDERING ONE MEDIUM SIZED TORTILA WEIGHING APP. 30 GMS [1 SERVING] WITH THE STUFFING

Method :

Take the boiled chickpea without water and smush or make it into chunks and mix with tahini, garlic, salt, and oil in a bowl, take tortillas, put in tahini mixture, jalapeno, lettuce, salsa, onion rings, and wrap it, heat in micro wave for 30 seconds and it's ready eat.

Gold Ball

Ingredients :

Cooking time : 25 to 30 minutes

- 3 russet or red potatoes
- 10 white bread slices
- Some amount plain bread crumbs
- 2 teaspoon sesame seeds
- 3 oz fresh coconut finely grated
- ½ oz broken cashew nut
- Some amount of golden raisin
- ½ oz crust raw peanuts
- Lemon drop to taste
- Sugar to taste
- ½ teaspoon green chili chopped
- ½ teaspoon garlic chopped
- ½ teaspoon ginger paste
- Pinch of kitchen king
- 3 oz finely chopped fresh cilantro
- Canola oil to deep fry

Apple butter sauce Ingredients: Some amount of red chili powder, salt to taste, and some amount of cumin powder, then mix well all together.

Method :

Boil potatoes very well. Peel skin out from potatoes and mash them in a bowl. Then put all other ingredients besides the bread slices in. Mix them well by your fingertips and make as many round balls as you can with your palms. Set all the balls in one plate. Remember; make the ball sizes small enough to fit in a bread slice. Wet the bread slice in water. Then squeeze water from bread slice by your palm. Put ball in middle and sat the bread slice all over to the ball by fingertips and coat it with breadcrumbs then set the ball in the plate. Heat oil in a saucepan at 375 degrees F then put the balls to fry, fry them until they are crispy and brown. Bring the balls out of the oil and serve them hot with apple butter sauce or green onion dip.

M.I.M Chunky Mix

Ingredients :

- 15 oz can boiled cheek pea
- 3 flour tortilla deep fried peaces
- 3 medium red potatoes boiled pieces
- Fresh mint deep to test
- Apple butter sauce to taste
- Red chili pepper
- Some amount of cumin powder
- Some amount of sesame tahini to taste
- 1 oz finely chopped onions

Fixing time :

8 to 10 minutes

Method :

Mix everything together real good. Sprinkle some red chili powder and it's ready to eat. You guys might be wondering what this name stands for it stands for:

- M - Mexico
- I - India
- M - Middle East

French Fried Sandwich

Ingredients :

- 1 long French bread
- 1 large French fries
- 2-teaspoon ketchup
- 2-teaspoon mayonnaise
- Hot sauce to taste
- 1 medium chopped onion
- 1 tablespoon dried Parmesan cheese
- Some amount fried onions
- 1-teaspoon creamy mustard blend
- Some amount lettuce cut

Fixing time :
5 minutes

Nutritive Value

ENERGY	- 670.0	KCAL
PROTEIN	- 9.6	GMS
FAT	- 7.5	GMS
FIBRE	- 1.0	GMS
SODIUM	- 22.0	MGMS
CALCIUM	- 98	MGMS
IRON	- 2.0	MGS
CARBOHYDRATES	- 75.0	GMS

THIS ABOVE RECIPE CONSIDERING ONE FRENCH BREAD WEIGHING APP. 100 GMS WITH THE FILLING

Method :

Take one long French bread, and cut it in half from the middle down. Combine all the remaining ingredients in one bowl, and then mix them together with the fries. Make sure it is all mixed properly. Then fill up the bread with these fries. Now it's ready to eat.

Jamaica Jerk Chicken

Ingredients :

- 10 pieces of chicken leg quarter
- 2-teaspoon hot jerk sauce
- ½ teaspoon tandoori paste (Patak's brand)
- 2-teaspoon onion powder
- 2-teaspoon veggie oil

Cooking time :

15-20 minutes

Tip :

Make sure that the chicken is tender and throughly cooked before serving.

Method :

Wash the leg very well, dry them with paper towel, put in bowl, then put in jerk sauce, tandoori paste, onion powder, oil, mix this by hand, and marinate the chicken for two to three hours before you cook it (or marinate this overnight if possible), then cook this on grille or non-stick pan. Brush oil on them, serve with tomato deep or mint deep.

Nutritive Value

ENERGY	-	185	KCAL
PROTEIN	-	13.0	GMS
FAT	-	10.6	GMS
FIBRE	-	0.0	GMS
SODIUM	-	0.2	MGMS
CALCIUM	-	13	MGMS
IRON	-	0.0	MGS
CARBOHYDRATES	-	2.0	GMS

THIS ABOVE RECIPE CONSIDERING ONE EACH QUARTER PIECE OF THE CHICKEN [1 SERVING] APP 100 GMS

Onion Omelet

Ingredients :

- 3 large eggs
- ¼ cup of milk
- 1 oz onion chopped
- Some amount of green onion cut
- Some amount of cilantro cut
- Pinch of red pepper
- ¼ teaspoon salt
- 2 clove garlic chopped
- ¼ teaspoon crust black pepper
- Crisco-butter flavored- no stick cooking spray

Fixing time :

5 minutes

Tips :

This can also serve with Ketchup or Maggi sauce

Method :

Whisk together all ingredients including the eggs in a bowl. 10 inch skillet generously with Crisco butter cooking spray, heat over medium, high heat until drop of water sizzles on it's surface, pour in egg mixture, tilt pan while pushing cooked portions toward the center with spatula, flip to the other side and after 2-3 seconds remove omelet by spatula and set in plate, serve hot with bread.

Rosemary Oven Lamb Leg

Ingredients :

- One leg of lamb (or same size beef or pork leg)
- 2-cup rosemary leaf chop
- 1 teaspoon Cajun spice seasoning
- ½ cup celery pieces
- 15-20-garlic cloves
- 1 oz sautéed onion
- ½ cup red wine
- 2/3-leaf chop fresh mint
- 1/4-cup olive oil
- Pinch of kitchen king seasoning
- Salt to taste
- 1/2-teaspoon crust black pepper
- 1-teaspoon butter or margarine
- 1 oven plastic bag to cook (or 1 foil tray with a foil cover)
- 2-teaspoon fresh squeezed lemon juice

Cooking time : 80-90 minutes

Method :

Use the point of a knife to make small pokes on the meat. Then, push garlic cloves and celery pieces in the openings of the meat. Then, put all the other ingredients in a bowl together and mix well. Take the oven plastic bag. Put the lamb leg in the bag and pour the red wine along with the mix in the bowl. Then, tie the bag. Keep it aside for about 2 hours to marinate it. After, preheat the oven to 400 degrees F. Set the bag in the tray, let it cook on 350 degrees F for 1 and ½ hours. Then, check the meat is tender. If not then cook it for a little more time. Now it is ready to eat.

Nutritive Value

ENERGY	- 517	KCAL
PROTEIN	- 21.7	GMS
FAT	- 43.6	GMS
FIBRE	- .01	GMS
SODIUM	- 1.1	MGMS
CALCIUM	- 25.1	MGMS
IRON	- 0.1	MGS
CARBOHYDRATES	- 4.0	GMS

THIS ABOVE RECIPE IS CONSIDERING VALUE OF ONE LEG OF THE LAMB [100 GMS] WITH THE GRAVY

Chicken Lollipops

Ingredients :

- 1 lb ground chicken
- 2 oz. bread crumbs
- 1 egg bitten
- ½ teaspoon finely chopped garlic
- Some amount of finely cut ginger
- Salt to taste
- Some sticks of fresh asparagus
- ½ teaspoon crust red pepper
- Canola oil to deep fry

Cooking time : 6-8 minutes
Preparation time : 6-8 minutes

Tips :

Before serving the Chicken Lollipops make sure the chicken is throughly cooked.

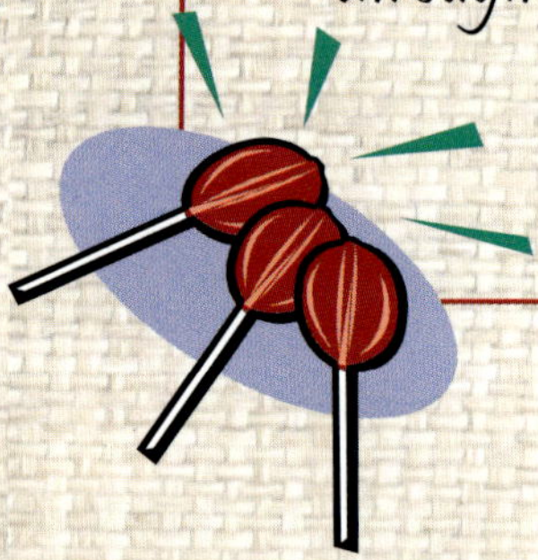

Method :

In one medium bowl put ground chicken, half amount of bread crumbs, egg, garlic, ginger, salt, red pepper and mix it very well by hand. Divide the mixture into ball shapes. Stick each ball to an asparagus stick. Put half amount of breadcrumbs in dine plate. Then roll over the lollipop in the breadcrumbs once. Heat oil in one medium saucepan to 375 degrees F. fill oil no more than half full with oil but deep enough for lollipop while it is frying. Avoid overcrowding. Frying them on medium heat until golden. Serve hot with dip or hot sauce.

Nutritive Value

ENERGY	-	450	KCAL
PROTEIN	-	37.7	GMS
FAT	-	45.0	GMS
FIBRE	-	13.0	GMS
SODIUM	-	5.0	MGMS
CALCIUM	-	34.5	MGMS
IRON	-	0.0	MGS
CARBOHYDRATES	-	2.0	GMS

THIS ABOVE RECIPIE CONSIDERING 150 GMS OF THE CHICKEN WITH THE OTHER ING [1 SERVING]

Lamb Cutlet

Ingredients :

- One lb lamb ground meat
  (beef or goat ground meat)
- 2 large boiled eggs chopped
- 2 or 3 petal mint chopped
- ½ teaspoon crust black pepper
- ½ teaspoon Cajun spice seasoning
- ¼ teaspoon ginger paste
- 3 cloves garlic chopped
- ½ teaspoon fresh lemon juice
- ½ teaspoon onion powder
- Canola oil to easy fry

Cooking time :
8-10 minutes

Method :

Mix all the ingredients besides, the oil with the ground meat in a mixing bowl. (Except oil) Divide the meat in a small ball with your palm and then press the ball. Make sure the shape is flat and round and only press it once. Keep them aside in a plate. Now heat a skillet on the stove and spread the oil with the spatula in the whole skillet. Put as many cutlets as you can or that will fit. Make both sides of the cutlet brown by medium temperature. Serve hot with mint dip and salad.

Toasty Parmesan Chicken Sub

Ingredients :

- 1 French bread long
- 1 lb grilled boneless chicken
- ¼ teaspoon crush pepper
- 5 slices pepper jack cheese
- 2 teaspoon dry parmesan cheese to sprinkle
- 2-or 3-tablespoon pizza sauce to spread
- Some amount of jalapeno slices
- Some amount of black olive slices
- Some amount of lettuce slices
- 2 teaspoon onion powder
- Some amount of olive oil

Fixing time :

6-8 minutes

Method :

Take French bread cut it in half down the middle, then spread pizza sauce on the bread, put on cheese slices, oil, then chicken slices, then set in a plate and set it in the toaster oven for while, bring it out. Put olive, parmesan cheese, crust pepper, jalapeno,onion powder, lettuce, and now it's ready to eat.

Crunchy Chinese Shrimp

Ingredients :

- 1 lb row shrimp with shell on
- 3-teaspoon potato starch
- ½ teaspoon soy sauce
- Lemon drop to taste
- 3 teaspoon melted butter
- Salt to taste
- Some amount of black pepper powder
- 1-teaspoon cumin powder
- Some amount of cilantro chopped
- ¼ teaspoon red chili powder
- Some amount of olive oil (to easily fry)
- ½ teaspoon garlic paste
- 1-teaspoon onion powder

Cooking time :

6-8 minutes

Nutritive Value

ENERGY	- 163 KCAL
PROTEIN	- 21 GMS
FAT	- 7.8 GMS
FIBRE	- 0.5 GMS
SODIUM	- 72.5 MGMS
CALCIUM	- 357 MGMS
IRON	- 5.8 MG
CARBOHYDRATES	- ------

THIS ABOVE VALUE IS FOR 110 GMS OF THE COOKED RECIPE PREPARATION

Method :

Wash shrimp with water and wrap them in paper towel for a while to squeeze the water and put them in one bowl with all upper ingredients, with melted butter without oil mix them, keep aside for about a half an hour before it is cooking, pour oil in one frying pan and heat it, put the shrimp in and cook them on a slow flame, do not cover while cooking, when they are cooked and golden brown then flip them on the other side, when the other side is golden brown it is ready to eat, Serve hottttt.

Fried Fish

Ingredients :

- 1 lb boneless fish cube
- 1 teaspoon of fish fried mix
- 1 teaspoon of fresh lemon squeeze
- Salt to taste
- ½ teaspoon cumin powder
- ½ teaspoon Cajun spice seasoning
- ¼ teaspoon red chili powder
- ¼ teaspoon garlic powder
- 1 teaspoon melted butter
- Vegetable oil to easily fry
- 1 oz chopped fresh cilantro

Cooking time :

6-10 minutes

Tips :

To make sure that all the fish cubes are about the same size and thickness. So that they cook evenly and when the fish is cooked through.

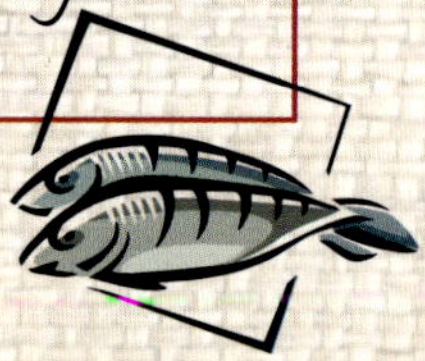

Method :

In one pot mix all the upper ingredients with fish cube and melted butter, heat non-stick skillet, spread oil by spatula on the whole surface, then put in fish cubes let it cook in medium heat, when the fishes bottom part becomes brown then center with spatula and flip to the other side, when other side is also brown then it is done, and it's ready to eat.

Green Mango Grilled Fish

Ingredients :

- 5 fillets of catfish boneless (or your favorite fish)
- 2 tablespoon finely chopped green mango
- ¼-teaspoon ground red pepper
- ¼-teaspoon salt
- ½-teaspoon cumin powder
- Some leaves of fresh mint chopped
- 1-tablespoon butter or oil
- ¼ teaspoon fresh limejuice
- ½ teaspoon breadcrumbs

Cooking time :

8-10 minutes

Nutritive Value

ENERGY	- 123	KCAL
PROTEIN	- 21.4	GMS
FAT	- 3	GMS
FIBRE	- NEGLIGIBLE	
SODIUM	- --------	
CALCIUM	- 10	MG
IRON	- --------	
CARBOHYDRATES	- 8.6	GMS

THIS ABOVE RECIPIE IS WEIGHING APP. 80 GMS. AND VIRGIN OIL INSTEAD OF BUTTER

Method :

Wash the fish fillet very good and keep them in paper towel, then pat dry. wrap until all water disappears, then combine all the remaining ingredients in one bowl, mix it and put the fish fillet in. Rub all spice mix on and marinate it for at least an hour before cooking. now heat grill skillet and put oil or butter on and put marinated fish on. let it cook on medium heat. Make them golden brown by flipping both sides. (if there is more oil to add then, you can always add in.) Serve hot.

Rosemary Grilled Lamb Chop

Ingredients :

- 1 lb lamb chop (goat chop or beef chop)
- 1 teaspoon meat tenderizer (brand- spice supreme)
- ½ teaspoon Cajun spice seasoning (brand- spice supreme)
- ½ teaspoon fresh rosemary cut
- 2 teaspoon brandy
- ¼ teaspoon crust pepper
- ¼ teaspoon canola oil
- ¼ teaspoon finely chopped ginger
- 1 teaspoon Heinz 57 Sauce

Cooking time :

20-30 minutes

Tips :

Before serving the Chop, make sure the Chop is tender and well cooked.

Method :

Put lamb chop and all remaining ingredients in one bowl and mix well by hand. Cover and marinate for overnight in refrigerator or marinate it for three hours before cooking it. Cook on grill or charcoal grill with a covered until the chop is tender. Serve hot!

Hakka Noodles

Ingredients :

- 10 oz thin chow main noodles
- 2 oz olive oil
- 1 bunch green onion cut
- 1 lb cabbage cut
- 3 oz mushroom cut
- 4 oz thin carrot slices
- Some amount of green and
- red bell pepper slices
- 1 large onion slices
- Some amount of spinach leaves

Cooking time : 10-15 minutes

- ½ teaspoon ginger chopped
- Some amount of celery chopped
- ½ teaspoon garlic chopped
- 2 tablespoon soya sauce
- Some amount of stir fry sauce
- Some amount of cilantro cut
- ¼ teaspoon glutamate

Method :

Put the noodles in boiling water and cook it for ½ minutes stirring occasionally. Flush noodle with cold water and drain. Heat oil in a skillet. Throw in onions, ginger, and garlic in. add all kinds of sauces in the recipe, and stir it. Then, put vegetables and noodles. Stir it on high flame for 2-3 minutes. If you need to add a little more oil, go ahead and do it. After, remove from heat and serve hot.

Nutritive Value

ENERGY	- 274 KCAL
PROTEIN	- 6.4 GMS
FAT	- 9.1 GMS
FIBRE	- 1.9 GMS
SODIUM	- 7.6 MGMS
CALCIUM	- 62.7 MGMS
IRON	- 2.2 MG
CARBOHYDRATES	- 39.4 GMS

THIS ABOVE VALUE IS FOR 150 GMS (1SERVING)OF THE COOKED RECIPE PREPARATION

Black Beans Bowl

Ingredients :

- 15 oz can black beans boiled
- 15 oz can kidney beans boiled
- 15 oz tomato puree
- 5 oz ultra pasteurized cream
- 1½ oz canola oil
- 2 teaspoon butter
- 1 large onion finely chopped
- ½ teaspoon ginger chopped
- 2 cloves garlic chopped
- ¼ teaspoon lemon juice
- ¼ teaspoon red chili powder
- ¼ teaspoon red chili powder
- 1-teaspoon cumin powder
- Pinch of kitchen king
- 2 beliefs
- Salt to taste

Cooking time :

10-15 minutes

Method :

Heat saucepan on medium heat, pour in oil and butter. Put in belief and make it brown. Put in onion and caramelize, add garlic and ginger, sauté for a minute. Put in black bean and kidney beans, tomato puree, uncover and cook for 5 minute. Put in red chili powder, salt, lemon, cumin powder, kitchen king, and simmer for 2 minutes, then add cream, stir and remove from heat. Srve hot with steamed basmati rice.

Creamy Mushrooms With Green Peas

Ingredients :

- 1 lb green peas
- 6 oz fresh slices mushroom
- 2 oz bell pepper slices
- Some amount of cashew nut
- ½ teaspoon red chili powder
- 2 oz cream
- Small amount of (reduced fat) feta cheese crank
- 1 teaspoon garlic paste
- 2 oz grinded onions
- 1 teaspoon cumin ground

Cooking time : around 30 minutes

- Pinch of kitchen king
- Cut cilantro to sprinkle on the top
- Salt to taste
- 16 oz tomato puree
- Lemon juice to taste
- 1 teaspoon garlic powder
- 2 oz olive oil
- 1 teaspoon butter
- 2 belief

Method :

Heat oil in vessel, put belief and cashew nut in; make a little golden, then put in onions, put ginger, garlic, tomato paste, peas, chili powder, cumin powder, salt, lemon juice, stir and cover the vessel, cook this for 10 minutes on medium temperature. Every five minutes open the lid and stir in and let it cook 75%.

Stir Fry :

Heat the frying pan and put in butter, put in mushroom and bell pepper slices. Sauté them on high flame for 2 minutes, then mix them with peas, and cream and stir it, cook until it first bubbles, remove from the stove, finally sprinkle cilantro and feta. Serve hot with rice, pita, or naan.

Tips :

Feel free to put in fat free sour cream beaten to taste instead of feta cheese if you do not like.

Nutritive Value

ENERGY	- 292.5	KCAL
PROTEIN	- 8.2	GMS
FAT	- 20.7	GMS
FIBRE	- 3.6	GMS
SODIUM	- 13.9	MGMS
CALCIUM	- 68.1	MGMS
IRON	- 1.7	MG
CARBOHYDRATES	- 16.9	GMS

THIS ABOVE VALUE IS FOR 150 GMS OF THE COOKED RECIPE PREPARATION

Whole Lenten Curry

Ingredients :

- 1 lb whole Lenten
- 1 large onion cut
- 1 large tomato cut
- 1/2-teaspoon ginger chopped
- 2 cloves garlic chopped
- Salt to taste
- Lemon squeeze drop to test
- 1/4 teaspoon red chili powder
- 1 oz peanut oil
- 1-teaspoon butter
- Pinch of kitchen king
- 1-teaspoon cumin powder
- 1/2-cup water

Cooking time :

15-20 minutes

Method :

Soak Lenten in tap water for at least two hours before cooking, heat vessel to the stove than pour oil and butter, heat it. Then sauté onion for while until golden brown, sauté garlic and ginger for a while, add tomato and stir for a while. Put chili and cumin powder, lemon drop and salt. Stir! Then add soaked Lenten with half cup of water and stir. Cover the vessel let it cook on medium flame. While it is cooking stir this in between time. (If you have turmeric powder in handy then put in 1/4 of the teaspoon). If you think ! that it is necessary to add more water than go ahead and add it. If Lenten is tender then it is cooked. Serve hottttttt with rice.

Cabbage Stir Fry

Ingredients :

- 1 lb cut cabbage
- 2 Medium red potatoes cut
- 3-teaspoon sesame seeds
- 1 green bell pepper slices
- 1 jalapeno chopped
- 1-teaspoon garlic ginger paste
- 1-teaspoon cumin powder
- Salt to test
- Fresh cilantro cut, or two teaspoon
- 1-tablespoon canola oil
- Few drops lemon squeeze

Cooking time :

10 minutes

Method :

Heat oil in a saucepan, put potatoes in, cover, and cook on high flame for 2-4 minutes. Then add all the left over ingredients in the list. Stir while this is cooking. Do not cover when it is done serve hot with bread.

Rowly Bowly Eggs Curry

Ingredients :

- 6 eggs
- 1 medium red onion chopped
- 1 medium ripe tomato chopped
- 1-tablespoon fresh cilantro cut
- 1-teaspoon garlic and ginger paste
- 1 teaspoon red chili powder
- 1-teaspoon cumin powder
- Pinch of kitchen king
- Salt to taste
- Lemon juice to taste

Cooking time :

25-30 minutes

- 1-tablespoon peanut oil
- 1-cup water
- 2-teaspoon tomato puree
- 2 cinnamon sticks
- 3 whole cloves
- 2 beliefs
- 1-drop anise extract
- 14-½ oz chicken broth

Method :

Heat the sauce pan on the stove, pour oil and heat, put in onions and make them caramelized, put in the tomatoes and sauté for 2 minutes, add all the upper ingredients except kitchen king and cilantro, stir them very well, put in water and chicken broth, cover the pan, cook on high flame for 5 minutes, open it up, if the water boils then crack the egg and put it in one by one, leave space between one by one and remember not to stir after eggs are in, cover the pan and let them cook on low flame for 15 minutes, open the cover and then stir them slowly, check if they are cooked if not then cover them back up and let them cook for a few more minutes, once these eggs are cooked sprinkle cilantro, and kitchen king, then stir. Serve this hot with basamati rice, pita, tortilla, or chapati.

Nutritive Value

ENERGY	- 188.5	KCAL
PROTEIN	- 9.1	GMS
FAT	- 11.9	GMS
FIBRE	- 0.1	GMS
SODIUM	- 3.4	MGMS
CALCIUM	- 49.2	MGMS
IRON	- 1.5	MG
CARBOHYDRATES	- 1.4	GMS

THIS ABOVE RECIPE CONSIDERING 1 EGG WITH CURRY - (1 SERVING)

Rowly Bowly Fried Eggs

Ingredients :

Cooking time : 8-10 minutes

- 4 raw eggs
- 3 eggs hard boiled and cut
- Large onion chopped
- Large fresh tomato chopped
- ½ teaspoon cumin powder
- Pinch of kitchen king
- ¼ teaspoon red chili powder
- ½ teaspoon garlic paste
- 1 hot green pepper chopped
- Salt to taste
- Few drops fresh lemon juice
- 1 oz vegetable oil
- 1 tablespoon green onion cut
- 1 teaspoon cilantro cut
- ½ teaspoon butter

Method :

Heat the fry pan on the stove. Put oil, butter, and heat it. Put chopped onion and stir it for about 2 minutes. Put the tomatoes and stir it for 3 minutes. Then, put garlic paste and stir for 1 minute, crack the raw eggs in and stir it for 2 minutes. Add other spices except the green onion and cilantro. Stir it well and add the cut boiled eggs and stir it for a while and last sprinkle the green onion and cilantro on top of it. Serve this hot with garlic bread or plain bread.

Nutritive Value

ENERGY	- 256.8	KCAL
PROTEIN	- 13.5	GMS
FAT	- 20.8	GMS
FIBRE	- 0.3	GMS
SODIUM	- 3.9	MGMS
CALCIUM	- 120.2	MGMS
IRON	- 1.5	MG
CARBOHYDRATES	- 4.8	GMS

THIS ABOVE RECIPE CONSIDERING ONLY 1 EGG (1 SERVING)

Soupy Chicken

Ingredients :

- 1 whole chicken pieces (skin off) 3 or 4 pounds
- 1 red (medium) onion chopped
- 5 medium fresh tomatoes chopped
- 1 oz canola oil
- Salt to taste
- 2-teaspoon cumin powder
- 2-teaspoon garlic paste
- 1 teaspoon ginger paste
- 2 teaspoon grated coconut
- 5-6 whole clove
- Cinnamon sticks
- 5 to 6 whole green cardamom
- 8 to 10 whole black pepper
- ¼ teaspoon kitchen king
- 1-tablespoon fresh chopped cilantro

Cooking time :

25-30 minutes

Tip :

Add 1/4 teaspoon of celery seeds in while it is cooking (if available) for a much more better taste.

Method :

Pour oil in one pot and heat it, put in whole clove, cinnamon stick, cardamom and make brown, put in chopped onions and make them golden brown, put in ginger, garlic paste and stir, put in chicken and saute for 2 minutes, put on spices, tomatoes, stir and cover. After 5 minutes add 2 cups of water and rest of the ingredients, cook until chicken is tender, garnish chicken with cilantro when it's time to serve, Serve with steamed basmati rice, serve with pita bread, pudo and with black salt salad.

Colorful Chicken Curry

Ingredients :

- 3 chicken legs, 3 chicken wings,
- or 3-split chicken breast
  1-teaspoon butter
- 1 oz peanut oil
- 2 medium red onion chop
- 1 medium yellow onion cut in big pieces
- 3 medium tomatoes cut
- 1 teaspoon chopped garlic
- 1 teaspoon chopped ginger
- Salt to taste
- 1-tablespoon grated fresh coconut
- 5 belief and cinnamon sticks
- 1-cup plain yogurt

Cooking time : 30-35 minutes

- ½ cup cut green onions
- 1 medium soup bowl mix chilly pieces (green, yellow, and red bell pepper)
- 2-tablespoon oil to stir-fry
- ½ bunch cut cilantro
- ½ teaspoon hot red chili
- 2 teaspoons cumin powder
- ½ teaspoon curry powder
- ¼ teaspoon kitchen king
- 1-teaspoon fresh lemon juice
- ½ teaspoon fennel seeds
- 2 drops red food coloring

Stir fry :

Heat the oil in another sauce pan, fry mix chili until half tender, keep aside in a plate, fry the cut onion until they're a little tender, and sprinkle stir fry chilies with cilantro on top of the cooked chicken, serve hot with basmati rice, your favorite bread, or salad.

Method :

Wash the chicken, put in lemon juice, ginger garlic paste, salt, chili powder, and curry powder mix and marinate 1 hour. Heat the vessel to the stove, pour oil and butter, put in chopped onions and coconuts to stir make it golden brown. Put in chicken for 5 to 7 minutes. Put the cut tomatoes stir for 2 minutes. Put all upper spices and yogurt (except the mix chili, cilantro, and green onions), stir them covered, and let it cook for 10 minutes. Check the Chicken, stir and cover for 10 minutes. Stir the chicken if cooked, remove it from the heat.

Green Chicken

Ingredients :

- 1 lb split skinless chicken breast
- 1 bunch spinach cut
- ½ oz fresh Ross merry leaf chopped
- 2 oz green onion chopped
- 1 oz green bell pepper chopped
- 5 oz plain yogurt
- 1 oz vegetable oil
- 1 teaspoon butter
- ½ teaspoon salt
- ½ teaspoon cumin powder
- ½ teaspoon hot green pepper chopped
- 3 clove garlic chopped
- 1 oz onion chopped
- 1 teaspoon fresh lemon juice

Cooking time : 30 minutes

Method :

Put chicken breast in one bowl, put in yogurt and salt, let this marinate for at least one hour before cooking, heat oil and butter in sauce pan, put in chopped onions and sauté for 1 minute, put marinated chicken in after 1 minute, now put all the rest of the ingredients with spinach, stir it covered and let it simmer until the chicken is tender, remove from the heat, serve this hot with basmati steamed rice, naan, or pita bread.

Nutritive Value

ENERGY	- 254.3	KCAL
PROTEIN	- 30.6	GMS
FAT	- 10.6	GMS
FIBRE	- 0.4	GMS
SODIUM	- 33.2	MGMS
CALCIUM	- 116.3	MGMS
IRON	- 0.9	MG
CARBOHYDRATES	- 5.2	GMS

THIS ABOVE RECIPIE IS FOR **150 GMS** OF THE COOKED RECIPIE PREPARATION

Thai Low Cocktail Seafood

Ingredients :

- 1 lb king crab leg
- 1 lb medium sized shrimp raw,
- 1 lb medium size shrimp raw peeled with the tail on
- ½ lb boneless fish cube
- 8 oz. of tomato puree
- 1 medium tomato chopped
- 2 oz. coconut milk
- 1 teaspoon garlic minced
- ¼ teaspoon ginger paste
- Sea salt to taste
- 1 ½ oz. sesame oil
- 1 teaspoon soy sauce
- ¼ teaspoon hot sauce
- ¼ teaspoon curry powder (asian or thai)
- ¼ teaspoon roasted cumin powder
- Fresh lemon drops to taste
- Fist amount of fresh cilantro cut
- 1 oz. water
- 3 bay leafs

Cooking time :

20 minutes

Method :

Heat oil in a saucepan. Put bay leafs, tomato puree and tomato chopped. Stir for one minute, put garlic, ginger, soy sauce, and hot sauce, stir for one minute. Add the crab legs and shrimp, stir for 2 minutes. Add coconut milk, salt, cumin powder, curry powder, lemon juice, and water, stir it. Cover and simmer it on medium flame. Until it is tender. Now add fish cubes, stir. Simmer until fish is tender. Remove from the heat and sprinkle cilantro on top. Serve hot with steamed parboiled rice.

Nutritive Value

ENERGY	-	6500	KCAL
PROTEIN	-	100	GMS
FAT	-	28.6	GMS
FIBRE	-	0.1	GMS
SODIUM	-	5.8	MGMS
CALCIUM	-	5964	MGMS
IRON	-	1.7	GMS
CARBOHYDRATES	-	9.9	GMS

THIS ABOVE RECIPE IS FOR 250 GMS (1SERVING) OF THE COOKED RECEIPE

7 Star of Green Beans

Ingredients :

- 5 oz. French green beans cut
- 2 oz. green peas
- 2 oz. green lima beans
- ½ lb baby eggplant cut
- 1 ripe banana cut with its skin still there
- ½ pound red potato cut
- ½ lb sweet potato cut
- 2 oz. roasted peanuts
- 1-teaspoon celery seeds
- ⅓-teaspoon salt (optional)
- ½ teaspoon cumin powder
- 3 cloves garlic minced
- 1 oz. vegetable oil
- 2 teaspoon margarine
- 1 oz. fresh cilantro cut
- 2 whole green jalapeno chopped
- Pinch of kitchen king

Cooking time :

15-20 minutes

Tip :

Feel free to add fresh soy beans in if you would like to add.

Variation :

Use sweet potatoes and ripe bananas to give the dish a delicately Sweet Flavour.

Method :

Take one oven tray big enough to fit easily all upper ingredients. Put all of them in a tray. Except oil, celery seeds and cilantro. Now, heat oil in a saucepan. Then, put celery seeds in. when they turn brown then remove from the heat. And put the vegetables into tray. Now mix them all by spatula and cover. Preheat the oven at 375 degrees F and let it cook with cover. In between time keep an eye on it. When all the vegetables are tender remove them from the oven. Sprinkle the cilantro on top. Serve hot.

Cheesy Broccoli With Egg

Ingredients :

- 1 lb broccoli pieces
- 4 eggs
- Some amount of mexican cheese
- 2 fresh green chili slices
- ½ teaspoon garlic chopped
- 1 oz olive oil
- 1-teaspoon butter
- ¼ teaspoon crushed black pepper
- Salt to taste
- Some amount of cut cilantro to sprinkle

Cooking time :

5-8 minutes

Method :

Pour oil and butter in a non-stick saucepan. Heat it. Put in garlic and sauté for a while, then put in broccoli, eggs, salt, chilli, crust pepper and stir. Don't over cook, place into a plate then sprinkle cheese and cilantro on it, then put it in the microwave for 1 minute. Now it's ready to eat.

Sesame Okra Fry

Ingredients :

- 1 lb fresh okra cut
- 1 oz fine corn flour
- 1 oz peanut oil
- 1 oz margarine
- 4-teaspoon brown sesame seeds
- ½ teaspoon salt
- 1-teaspoon cumin powder
- ¼ teaspoon crust black pepper
- Red chili powder to taste
- 1-teaspoon crust garlic

Cooking time :
8-10 minutes

Tips :

When you buy Okra, make sure they are not shriveled and that they do not have any brown spots, Okra naturally thickness curries and casseroles.

Method :

Pour oil in saucepan, heat on the stove, put okra in, stir once and cover, after 2 minutes uncover it, add all the upper ingredients with margarine and corn flour, constantly stir very well and let it be on medium temperature, when the okra looks tender and crispy then it's ready to eat.

Colorful Chickpea

Ingredients :

- 15 oz boiled chickpea
- 1 large onion cut
- 1-teaspoon garlic chopped
- 1 large fresh tomato cut
- ½ oz vegetable oil
- ½ teaspoon margarine
- ¼ teaspoon salt
- 4 whole clove
- 1 stick cinnamon
- 3 beliefs
- ½ teaspoon cumin powder
- Some amount of parsley or cut cilantro
- Fresh lemon drops to taste

Cooking time :

5 minutes

Tips :

Feel free to add a little amount of chopped sweet basil to taste

Method :

Heat oil in saucepan, crackle the clove, cinnamon, belief, then add onion and garlic, sauté for 2 minutes, then add all the left over ingredients with chickpea, (add chickpea without water) stir this for 2 minutes, sprinkle cilantro on top, then it's ready to serve with rice or bread.

Chipotle Chicken Low

Ingredients :

- 1 lb boneless chicken strips
- 2 oz nonfat sour cream
- 2 cloves garlic chopped
- ½ teaspoon salt
- ½ teaspoon chipotle ground red pepper
- Pinch of saffron thread
- 1-teaspoon fresh lemon juice
- ½ teaspoon ginger chopped
- 2-tablespoon olive oil
- 2-teaspoon margarine
  (I cant believe it isn't butter)
- ½ teaspoon whole cumin
- 1 oz green onion cut
- Some amount of onion pieces
- Some of red, yellow, and green bell pepper slices

Cooking time : 10-15 minutes

Nutritive Value

ENERGY	- 316.2	KCAL
PROTEIN	- 43.7	GMS
FAT	- 1.4	GMS
FIBRE	- 0.1	GMS
SODIUM	- 0.2	MGMS
CALCIUM	- 43.9	MGMS
IRON	- 0.4	MG
CARBOHYDRATES	- 6.8	GMS

THIS ABOVE RECIPE IS FOR 125 GMS (1 SERVING) OF THE COOKED RECEIPE PREPARATION

Method :

Put chicken strips in a bowl; with the strips combine all ingredients except oil, margarine, onion cut, and bell pepper slices. Mix the chicken very well and leave it aside for about 2 hours to marinate. Now heat the skillet to the stove. Put oil in and chicken and let it cook on medium flame. While it is cooking keep your eyes on the chicken. When one side of the chicken is cooked, you can flip it before it gets burnt. Then add onion, bell pepper and margarine and let them cook all together for 2-3 minutes. After, stir it with a spatula and remove it from the heat. Garnish with green onion and serve hot.

Couscous of Low

Ingredients :

- 5 oz couscous pack
  (Brand- Hodgson mill- with miled flax seed & soy)
- 2 oz onion cut
- 1 oz tomatilo cut
- 1 oz sun dried tomato cut
- 1 teaspoon ketchup
- ¼ teaspoon whole cumin seeds
- 2 teaspoon white poppy seeds
- 3 eggs of egg white beaten
- ½ teaspoon red crust pepper
- 3 cloves garlic chopped
- 1 oz extra virgin olive oil or margarine
  (I recommended "I can not believe it's not butter")
- 1 oz cabbage cut
- ¼ teaspoon salt

Cooking time :
8 minutes

Method :

Put oil or margarine in medium saucepan, heat it, put onion and caramelized, then add beaten eggs, stir for a little, then put in all the remaining ingredients, add water as it says on the couscous pack, then follow the pack directions.

Nutritive Value

ENERGY	- 453	KCAL
PROTEIN	- 17.5	GMS
FAT	- 6.7	GMS
FIBRE	- 20.5	GMS
SODIUM	- 3.6	MGMS
CALCIUM	- 119.2	MGMS
IRON	- 4.2	MG
CARBOHYDRATES	- 47.4	GMS

THIS ABOVE RECIPE IS FOR 150 GMS OF THE COOKED PREPARATION AND CONSIDERING VIRGIN OIL INSTEAD OF MARGARINE

Basil Pesto Rice

Ingredients :

- 100-ml. brown basmati rice
- 700-ml. water
- 150 ml nonfat plain yogurt
- 2 oz. nonfat sour cream
- ½ teaspoon sea salt
- ½ teaspoon ginger paste
- 3 cloves garlic peeled
- 2 oz. fresh basil leaves
- 1 tablespoon margarine
- 1 oz. canola oil
- 1 tablespoon black sesame seeds
- 1 teaspoon red lentil
- 2 oz. diced onion
- 3 whole dried hot red chilies
- Fresh hot green pepper or fresh jalupeno
- 1 teaspoon fresh lemon juice

Cooking time : 25-30 minutes

Method :

RICE:
Bring water to boil in one medium pot and put brown rice in. put the salt in. cover and simmer it at medium heat. keep an eye and stirring occasionally. Let it fully cook.

Toping :

Heat oil in a small saucepan. Break dry chili, put them in and let it black brown. Then put black sesame seeds, red lentil, diced onion and make them golden brown. Remove from the heat.

Mix :

Now whisk the yogurt in a bowl and put in the cooked rice. Stir well. Put the sesame toping on and stir it. Remove the rice from the heat. (Remember this rice has to be sticky. If there is more water needed, add some more water in.)

Basil Pesto :

Put basil leaves, sea salt, green chili, garlic, ginger, lemon juice in a food processor. Run only for three to four times. Do not make it very fine.

Serving :

Serve the cooked rice in the plate and put some basil pesto in. Stir it, eat it right a way.

Nutritive Value

ENERGY	- 779	KCAL
PROTEIN	- 8.0	GMS
FAT	- 3.0	GMS
FIBRE	- 25.1	GMS
SODIUM	- 25.0	MGMS
CALCIUM	- 238.0	MGMS
IRON	- 1.3	GMS
CARBOHYDRATES	- 50.3	GMS

THIS ABOVE RECIPE IS FOR 150 GMS (1SERVING) OF THE COOKED RECEIPE

Rice A Roni ; Creamy Four Cheese

Ingredients :

- 1 package of 4.8 oz rice a roni creamy four cheese
- 1 lb broccoli bud
- 2 oz mushroom slices
- 1 oz green onion cut
- 1 oz yellow onion cut
- 1 oz bell pepper cut (green, yellow, red)
- ½ teaspoon of red crust pepper
- 3 oz carrot cut
- 3 tablespoon margarine

Cooking time : 30 minutes

Method :

In a skillet caramelize all vegetables with one tablespoon of margarine and keep aside in one plate. Then follow package direction putting "Rice A Roni" in the skillet. [When skillet is covered that time add the caramelize vegetable in].

Bombay Mutton Biriyani

Ingredients :

- 2 lb goat meat (mutton) pieces (or beef or pork meat)
- 2-cup basmati rice
- ½ cup whole lentil
- 4 hard boiled eggs slices
- Medium bell pepper slices stir-fried
- 1 large onion chopped
- ½ cup fried onions
- 1 medium potato slices fried
- 1 medium tomato slices
- 1-teaspoon tomato puree
- Salt to taste
- Lemon juice to taste
- ½ cup coconut milk
- Pinch of saffron
- 3 clove
- 3 cinnamon sticks
- 3 beliefs
- 6 whole green cardamoms
- 3 black cardamom
- 1-teaspoon red chili powder
- 1-teaspoon black pepper powder
- 1 ½ teaspoon ginger chopped
- 1-teaspoon garlic chopped
- 2-teaspoon cumin powder
- ½ teaspoon kitchen king
- ½ cup cilantro
- 1 oz green onion cut
- 2 oz canola oil
- 1 oz butter or margarine
- 2 leaves fresh mints chopped
- 1/8 teaspoon mace powder

Cooking time : 1½ - 2 hours

Method : Meat

Wash the goat pieces; put in mace powder. Ginger, garlic, coconut milk and lemon juice marinate this for at least 2 hours. Heat up a non-stick vessel on the stove. Put oil in it. Butter, throw in clove, cinnamon sticks, belief, cardamom, black cardamom, let them crackle. Put in chopped onions and stir for a while. Now put in the marinated goat pieces, tomato, salt, chili, cumin, and black pepper powder. Stir for 5 minutes. Cover the vessel for 10 minutes. Check and stir again. Cover and let it cook on medium heat for 10 minutes. Add chopped mint, kitchen king, stir well, cover the vessel. Let it cook, while cooking when ever you feel like stirring. When the meat is tender remove vessel from the stove.

Rice :

Soak rice and Lenten in tab water for at least 1 hour, pour 10-12 cups of water, put on stove on high flame, cover, when the water boils add the rice and beans in the pot, cover, after one boil, uncover the pot and let them cook 75% then drain with a strainer, keep a side.

Saffron :

Take 3 teaspoon of milk. Warm it, put saffron. Mix this very well until it turn in yellow color.

Mixing :

Take one glass tray or other type of tray spread the cooked meat on the cooked rice with beans, spread tomatoes, potatoes, fried onions, fried bell pepper, slices of eggs, sprinkle cut green onion and green cilantro, same way layer as many that fit in tray, and finally spread the saffron milk all over the rice, cover tray, preheat the oven on 200F, put the tray in oven for 30 to 45 minutes, serve the biriyani hot with raita or salad.

Nutritive Value

ENERGY	- 591	KCAL
PROTEIN	- 39.2	GMS
FAI	- 18.3	GMS
FIBRE	- 0.3	GMS
SODIUM	- 48.4	MGMS
CALCIUM	- 3.8	MGMS
IRON	- 70.5	MGS
CARBOHYDRATES	- 3.3	GMS

THIS ABOVE RECIPE IS FOR 250 GMS (1SERVING) OF THE COOKED RECEIPE

Khichadi of India

Ingredients :

- ½ lb long grain rice
- ½ lb red lenten
- ½ lb eggplant cut
- 1 medium potato cut
- 2 medium tomatoes (ripe) chopped
- ½ lb sinqua cut
- 1 oz cabbage cut
- 1 oz french green beans
- 1 oz lima beans
- 1 oz green peas
- 1 oz raw peanut
- 1 oz cashew nut
- 1 medium onion sliced
- 2 teaspoon whole cumin seeds
- 3 cloves
- 1 belief
- 1 cinnamon stick
- Some amount of cilantro cut
- Some amount of green onions cut
- ¼ teaspoon turmeric powder
- ¼ teaspoon red chili powder
- 1/3 teaspoon of salt
- ½ teaspoon garlic chopped
- 2-teaspoon butter
- 2 oz peanut oil
- 4 cup of water

Cooking time :

30-40 minutes

Tips :

Instead of serving plain buttermilk, add in roasted cumin powder, fresh chopped, cilantro, salt, sugar and hot green chillies paste to taste and stir.

Method :

Wash rice and lenten, soak at least 1 hour before it's cooked, heat oil and butter in one saucepan, throw cloves, cinnamon and belief make them quite brown, put in onion slices, sauté them for 1 minute, then add tomatoes, sauté for 2 minutes, add all spices, ginger and garlic, then stir for a while, add all vegetables, stir for 2 minutes, then add rice with lenten and water, stir, simmer covered on slow temperature until this is tender. If you want to make khichadi more sticky, add more water, then simmer for a while. Serve hot with raita, salad or with butter milk.

Nutritive Value

ENERGY	-	638	KCAL
PROTEIN	-	21.2	GMS
FAT	-	21.3	GMS
FIBRE	-	2.2	GMS
SODIUM	-	32.6	MGMS
CALCIUM	-	98.0	MGMS
IRON	-	5.7	MGS
CARBOHYDRATES	-	88.8	GMS

THIS ABOVE RECIPE IS FOR 250 GMS (1SERVING) OF THE COOKED RECEIPE

Cauliflower Rice

Ingredients :

- 2 cups Basmati rice
- 1 oz fresh or frozen green peas
- 1 oz cut corn
- 1-teaspoon whole cumin seeds
- 1-tablespoon olive oil
- 1-teaspoon butter
- Salt to taste
- 2 hand-full broken cashews
- 3 green cardamom pods
- 2 bay leafs
- 2 whole cloves
- 1 cinnamon stick
- 8-10 black peppers
- 1 tablespoon fried onion
- 1 green chili slice
- 3 oz cauliflower pieces
- 2 ½ cups of water

Cooking time :

15-20 minutes

Method :

Wash rice with water. Put water and rice in the rice cooker pot. Put salt, peas, and corn. Set the bowl of rice in the rice cooker covered, then turn the switch on, while it cooks heat a saucepan on the stove, and heat oil and butter. Now, heat the saucepan on the stove. Heat oil and butter. Throw in the cardamom, cloves, bay leaves, and cinnamon. Make them brown. After, throw in cashews to make it golden. Add cumin seeds and chili slices. Stir it for a while and bring it to the rice cooker pot. Then, add in the rice. Also add the cauliflower. Stir once and cover the pot. Let it cook. Serve hot with favorite raita or serve with buttermilk.

Buttermilk- add small amount of cilantro paste, a pinch of cumin powder, salt, and sugar to taste. Stir it and serve.

Pudo

Ingredients :

- 2-cup fine rice flour
- ½ cup wheat fine flour
- Non-stick cooking spray oil
- 1-teaspoon salt

Cooking time :
around 2 minutes

Method :

Combine rice flour, wheat flour & salt in one bowl. Pour around 5-6 cups of tab water. Make the batter in smooth consistency. At least make the batter 2 hours before preparing it. Heat the non-stick skillet on the stove by high flame. Spread no stick oil on the whole surface of the skillet. Pour the batter on the skillet with a grip spoon into a round shape. Cover until 30-40 seconds pass by, open the lid and wait until the steam goes away. The center of the spatula and flip it to the other side. Cook until other part is brown (or for 1 minute . Serve this with any soupy dish, like chicken curry, potato curry, or any hot curry.

Stuffed Date

Ingredients :

- 15 oz date (fat or thin)
- 5 oz honey
- 1-tablespoon creamy peanut butter
- 1 tablespoon clarified butter
- 2 oz white poppy seeds
- 5 oz crust almonds
- 2 pinch of fine nutmeg powder

Preparation time :

20-30 minutes

Method :

Mix- Put honey, peanut butter, clarified butter, crushed almonds, and nutmeg powder in one mixing bowl and mix it with spatula, now cut the date from the center, now discard the seed out and fill in the mixture .

Topping- Place the poppy seeds in the plate and roll the stuffed dates on tope of the poppy seeds. Now it's ready to eat.

Ginger Ale Mix

Ingredients :

- 12 oz chilled ginger ale
- 12 oz chilled club soda
- ¼ teaspoon black salt
- ½ teaspoon roasted cumin powder
- 3 pinch of freshly peppercorn ground
- Lime juice to taste

Fixing time :

1 minutes

Method :

In one glass put in lime juice, black salt, cumin powder, and stir well, then add the chilled ginger ale and club soda into the mix.

Variation :

This drink is good for you after a heavy meal to help with your digestion and fill stomach haaaaaaas). Trust me your tummy will thank you.

Romeo Mix

Ingredients :

- 4 oz 100% cranberry juice
- 2 oz 100% pomegranate juice
- 2 oz tomato juice
- 1 oz vodka (optional)
- 1-teaspoon fresh squeezed limejuice
- ¼ teaspoon freshly ground peppercorn (optional)
- Pinch of salt
- 1 scoop orange sherbet-frozen
- 1 cube ice

Preparation time :

2 minutes

Method :

Put all the following ingredients in blender except peppercorn, and frozen orange sherbet, run the electric blender four to five times until it is mixed well and pour it into a glass. Now top this with frozen orange sherbet and freshly ground peppercorn.

Fried Fruit Dessert

Ingredients :

- Ripe bananas
- Strawberries
- Apples
- Bisquick powder
- Pancake syrup to sprinkle
- Sugar powder to sprinkle
- Cinnamon powder to sprinkle
- Nutmeg powder to sprinkle
- Canola oil to deep fry

Cooking time :

5 minutes

Method :

Make batter ready one hour before cooking. First, put water and bisquick powder in a bowl and mix. (Make the better texture like pancake batter consistency) Pour oil in a saucepan or a deep fryer. Fill no more than half of it with oil. Make it deep enough for the food to float while frying and bring oil to 375degrees F heat. Peal off the skin from the fruits. Cut the fruits into thick slices. Dip slices one-by-one in the batter till well coated. Then, put it in oil very gently by your fingertips. Fry until it is golden, brown and then remove from the oil, set them into a plate. Finally, sprinkle them with a little sugar powder, cinnamon powder, nutmeg powder and pancake syrup.

Threadey Dessert

Ingredients :

- 4 oz finely thin vermicelli
- 2 ½ liter 2% milk
- 8 oz sweetened condensed milk
- 2 teaspoon clarified butter
- 1 oz almond slices
- ½ oz pistachio crust
- ¼ teaspoon nutmeg powder or even less
- Little amounts of saffron thread

Cooking time :

20-25 minutes

Tip :

To make more tasty, serve it with cut fruit as a banana, cantaloupe, honeydew, sapodilla, papaya, etc

Method :

Heat one nonstick saucepan on medium flame. Put clarified butter in. then, put vermicelli in and constantly stir it for one minute by the spatula and until it is golden. Pour milk in immediately, (keep stirring). One bubbling, add condensed milk and almond slices in. Keep stirring until the texture is a thick liquid. Remove it from the heat. After it is a little cooled, add nutmeg powder, pistachio and saffron in. Serve cold or warm.

Pancake Fruit dessert

Ingredients :

- 3 pancake normal size thin
- Pancake syrup
- 8 oz cool whip
- 2 oz heavy milk
- 1 or 2 drops vanilla extract
- Ripe banana chop ⅓ cup
- ½ cup strawberry, apple, pear chopped mixed
- 1 tablespoon walnut crank
- 2 oz banana pudding
- Unsalted butter to taste

Fixing time :

8-10 minutes

Method :

Make thin pancake in unsalted butter. Combine cool whip, heavy milk and vanilla extract. Stir well in one bowl. Sat 1 pancake in glass skillet, put pancake syrup on top of the pancake. Layer banana pudding, layer fruit and walnut. Then spread whip cream mix. Put on the remaining pancake and layer same way on top. Finally spread the whip cream and pour pancake syrup all over. Put some fruit, keep in refrigerator for minimum 5 to 6 hours. Now it's ready to eat.

Roasted Garlic

Ingredients :

Separate the garlic

Note :

Garlic is good for: blood pressure and cholesterol.

Tip

It can also serve as a starter with alcoholic drink.

Method :

Take one whole garlic bulb, burst the garlic clove each by hitting with wider side of the knife. Toss them putting it in with 1 teaspoon extra virgin olive oil. Put it in one covered pan on slow flame. Keep your eyes on it and stirring once. Also you can roast in oven on 375 degrees F. Until it becomes soft. Now remove it from the heat and peel the skin off. Eat it plain or sprinkle some red pepper powder, black pepper crust, salt, few drops of lemon juice or few drops of red wine vinegar, and cumin powder.

Index

Index

Conversion Table

1 ounce (OZ)	= 437.5 Grains = 28.35 G
1 pound (LB)	= 16 OZ = 0.4535 kg
1 fliud ounce (FL OZ)	= 2.95 cl
1/4 teaspoon	= 1 ML
1/2 teaspoon	= 2 ML
1 teaspoon	= 5 ML
1 tablespoon	= 12.5 ML
2 tablespoon	= 25 ML
1/4 Cup	= 62 ML
1/2 Cup	= 125 ML
3/4 Cup	= 190 ML
1 Cup	= 250 ML
1/3 Cup	= 83 ML

Authentic, delicious recipes of international flavor, for the enjoyment of family and friends.

Let me tell you something about myself. Since I was youny I have always loved to cook and help my mom and dad when they cooked in the kitchen. Then when I became a teen I started to make big meals for lunch and dinners all by myself to feed my family, guests, friends and many others. This became an interest over the years so then as years went by I enjoyed feeding my friends and family many new varieties of food. Food has helped me when family is together, and making new long and happy relationships. Food is the way I always enjoy my happy hours with my family and friends. I thought of writing this cookbook because many people have told me to open a restaurant, so many people could enjoy this type of food and then I thought to myself why do that when I could just bring home many of my recipes to many homes, I am sure you all will be Happy and Enjoy this simple & fun recipes with have lots of fun while cooking and having it all.

- Sadhana Mistry